AN ENGAGING
COMIC BOOK
JOURNAL

Introduction

Why does anyone need a journal?

Journals offer a creative way to document your life. No matter what your age, gender, ethnicity, religious or political beliefs, color of your skin or general physical appearance, writing can help anyone process feelings, build writing skills, and communicate ideas. It is a great way to explore yourself in a non-judgmental way.

We tend to notice the big things that happen each day, but many of the little things go unnoticed if we don't take the time to take note of them. Unfortunately, the things we notice aren't always pleasant. Writing down things that make you smile or frown every week can make you feel better about a difficult day.

It provides confidence in your ability to handle the challenges. You can revisit past weeks and look for patterns. It's often easier to understand the present if you can analyze the past. You can begin to learn what makes you happy. You can learn what makes you, you!

But what do you do if you're not the writing type or maybe you don't think you're creative? Journaling does not always involve writing. You can easily express your thoughts in different ways, such as drawing, sketching, or pasting pictures. Sometimes people just need more inspiration to start.

That's the idea of this journal - its looks and feels like a comic strip which is relaxing and inspiring. It provides many prompts to help give you an idea on what to write regarding Goal Planning, Managing Anxiety, Positive Thinking, Inspiration, List Making, Imaginative Thoughts, Creativity and Self Exploration.

I encourage you to not only write, but draw pictures, use lots of color or doodle a little every day or pick one day each week to highlight the many exciting things that occurred, both Good and Bad.

This is me!

My Name is: __Evan__

I am __11__ years old

I am a __girl__ !

I have __2__ eyes.

My height: __just right__

I have: ____ pets

I have:
- __✓__ long
- ____ medium
- ____ short
- ____ no hair.

Generally, I am:
- ____ calm
- __✓__ nervous
- ____ anxious
- __✓__ outgoing
- ____ shy
- ____ it changes each day
- ____ other

I am a:
- ____ child
- __✓__ pre-teen
- ____ Teenage
- ____ Adult
- ____ Senior

I have:
- ____ sisters
- __✓__ sisters I like
- ____ brothers
- __✓__ brothers I like

I am __awesome__

My weight: __is ideal for me__

I am __smart__ !

I have a job/career? Yes or (No)

Most days I like to dress?
- __✓__ casual
- ____ formal
- ____ comfortable
- ____ neat
- ____ one color
- ____ business
- ____ black
- ____ colorful
- ____ larger size than I need
- ------ smaller size than I should
- ____ whatever's clean
- ____ other?

I am perfect!

"What lies behind you and what lies in front of you, pales in comparison to what lies inside of you."
— Ralph Waldo Emerson

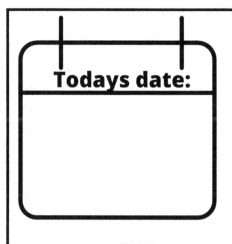

Todays date:

The next eight pages reflect my views and feelings for this past week.

What was the weather this week?

Anything exciting happen in the world this week?

Circle your emoji(s) for the week below or draw your own!

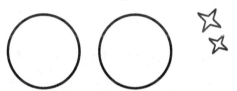

Action word of the week!

The moment I enjoyed the most -

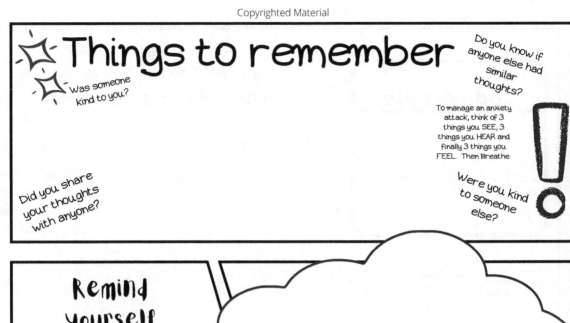

Things to remember

Was someone kind to you?

Do you know if anyone else had similar thoughts?

To manage an anxiety attack, think of 3 things you SEE, 3 things you HEAR and finally 3 things you FEEL. Then Breathe.

Did you share your thoughts with anyone?

Were you kind to someone else?

Remind yourself that it's OK not to be perfect!
- Unknown

My best thought ....

My worst thought ....

Believe

in

YOURSELF!!

You were given this life because you are strong enough to live it.

- Unknown

WOW!

These things made me happiest this week

How can I continue to be happy?

What went wrong this week?

Everyone wants happiness.
No one wants pain.
But you can't have a rainbow, without a little rain!
- Unknown

What can I do to make next week better?

Other things to note:

Could you have changed the outcome?

Who could have shared your joy or offered support?

Did you get support when or if you needed it?

Whether the sky is blue or gray, there is something to LOVE everyday!

- Unknown

SUNDAY TUESDAY

THURSDAY

Goals for next week!

FRIDAY

MONDAY

WEDNESDAY SATURDAY

Don't change so people like you, Be yourself and the right people will LOVE the real you!

- Unknown

- Read more
- cook a meal
- acheive 100% attendance
- clean your room
- ask a friend if they need help
- study an extra hour
- try a new hairstyle
- have a digital free evening at home
- try one new food item

- be kind to a stranger

- talk to one person outside your social group
- hug a parent

- say Hi to someone new!

YEAH

DESTROY THIS PAGE

Bad thoughts can inhabit you for weeks if you don't deal with them. Although they can be hard to deal with, occasional bad thoughts are normal and your brain has ways of dealing with them. In this method, you can deal with negative feelings by writing them down. But what do you do when you don't want anyone to read them?

You destroy them!

Life's problems wouldn't be called hurdles, if there wasn't a way to get over them.

- Unknown

Write your deepest, darkest thoughts and then destroy this page by either coloring over your writing or rip the page out and have fun destroying it in safe ways.

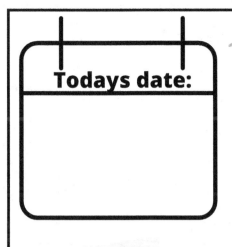

Todays date:

The next eight pages reflect my views and feelings for this past week.

What was the weather this week?

Anything exciting happen in the world this week?

Circle your emoji(s) for the week below or draw your own!

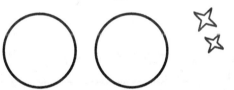

Action word of the week!

The moment I enjoyed the most -

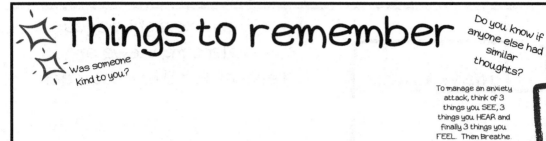

Things to remember

Was someone kind to you?

Do you know if anyone else had similar thoughts?

To manage an anxiety attack, think of 3 things you SEE, 3 things you HEAR and finally 3 things you FEEL. Then Breathe.

Did you share your thoughts with anyone?

Were you kind to someone else?

Remind yourself that it's OK not to be perfect!
- Unknown

My best thought ....

My worst thought ....

Believe

in

YOURSELF!!

You were given this life because you are strong enough to live it.

- Unknown

WOW!

These things made me happiest this week

How can I continue to be happy?

What went wrong this week?

Everyone wants happiness.
No one wants pain.
But you can't have a rainbow, without a little rain!

- Unknown

What can I do to make next week better?

Other things to note:

Could you have changed the outcome?

Who could have shared your joy or offered support?

Did you get support when or if you needed it?

whether the sky is blue or gray, there is something to LOVE everyday!

- Unknown

SUNDAY TUESDAY

THURSDAY

Goals for next week!

FRIDAY

MONDAY

WEDNESDAY SATURDAY

Don't change so people like you, Be yourself and the right people will LOVE the real you!

- Unknown

- Read more
- cook a meal
- acheive 100% attendance
- clean your room
- ask a friend if they need help
- study an extra hour
- try a new hairstyle
- have a digital free evening at home
- try one new food item
- be kind to a stranger
- talk to one person outside your social group
- hug a parent
- say Hi to someone new!

YEAH

DESTROY THIS PAGE

Bad thoughts can inhabit you for weeks if you don't deal with them. Although they can be hard to deal with, occasional bad thoughts are normal and your brain has ways of dealing with them. In this method, you can deal with negative feelings by writing them down. But what do you do when you don't want anyone to read them?

You destroy them!

Life's problems wouldn't be called hurdles, if there wasn't a way to get over them.

- Unknown

Write your deepest, darkest thoughts and then destroy this page by either coloring over your writing or rip the page out and have fun destroying it in safe ways.

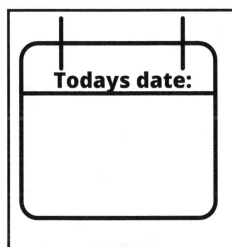

Todays date:

The next eight pages reflect my views and feelings for this past week.

What was the weather this week?

Anything exciting happen in the world this week?

Circle your emoji(s) for the week below or draw your own!

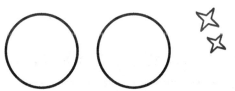

Action word of the week!

The moment I enjoyed the most -

✦ Things to remember

Was someone kind to you?

Do you know if anyone else had similar thoughts?

To manage an anxiety attack, think of 3 things you SEE, 3 things you HEAR and finally 3 things you FEEL. Then Breathe.

Did you share your thoughts with anyone?

Were you kind to someone else?

Remind yourself that it's OK not to be perfect!
- Unknown

My best thought ....

My worst thought ....

Believe

in

YOURSELF!!

You were given this life because you are strong enough to live it.

- Unknown

WOW!

These things made me happiest this week

How can I continue to be happy?

What went wrong this week?

Everyone wants happiness.
No one wants pain.
But you can't have a rainbow, without a little rain!
- Unknown

- _____

- _____

- _____

What can I do to make next week better?

- _____

- _____

- _____

Other things to note:

Could you have changed the outcome?

Who could have shared your joy or offered support?

Did you get support when or if you needed it?

Whether the sky is blue or gray, there is something to LOVE everyday!

- Unknown

Goals for next week!

SUNDAY TUESDAY THURSDAY FRIDAY MONDAY WEDNESDAY SATURDAY

Don't change so people like you, Be yourself and the right people will LOVE the real you!

- Unknown

- Read more
- cook a meal
- acheive 100% attendance
- clean your room
- ask a friend if they need help
- study an extra hour
- try a new hairstyle
- have a digital free evening at home
- try one new food item

- be kind to a stranger
- talk to one person outside your social group
- hug a parent
- say Hi to someone new!

YEAH

DESTROY THIS PAGE

Bad thoughts can inhabit you for weeks if you don't deal with them. Although they can be hard to deal with, occasional bad thoughts are normal and your brain has ways of dealing with them. In this method, you can deal with negative feelings by writing them down. But what do you do when you don't want anyone to read them?

You destroy them! ⟶

Life's problems wouldn't be called hurdles, if there wasn't a way to get over them.

– Unknown

Write your deepest, darkest thoughts and then destroy this page by either coloring over your writing or rip the page out and have fun destroying it in safe ways.

Todays date:

The next eight pages reflect my views and feelings for this past week.

What was the weather this week?

Anything exciting happen in the world this week?

Circle your emoji(s) for the week below or draw your own!

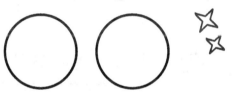

Action word of the week!

The moment I enjoyed the most -

Things to remember

Was someone kind to you?

Do you know if anyone else had similar thoughts?

To manage an anxiety attack, think of 3 things you SEE, 3 things you HEAR and finally 3 things you FEEL. Then Breathe.

Did you share your thoughts with anyone?

Were you kind to someone else?

Remind yourself that it's OK not to be perfect!

- Unknown

My best thought ....

My worst thought ....

Believe

in

YOURSELF!!

You were given this life because you are strong enough to live it.

- Unknown

WOW!

These things made me happiest this week

How can I continue to be happy?

What went
wrong this
week?

Everyone wants
happiness.
No one wants
pain.
But you can't
have a rainbow,
without a little
rain!
- Unknown

- _____

- _____

- _____

What can I do to
make next week
better?

- _____

- _____

- _____

Other things to note:

Could you have changed the outcome?

Who could have shared your joy or offered support?

Did you get support when or if you needed it?

Whether the sky is blue or gray, there is something to LOVE everyday!

- Unknown

Goals for next week!

SUNDAY
TUESDAY
THURSDAY
FRIDAY
MONDAY
SATURDAY
WEDNESDAY

Don't change so people like you, Be yourself and the right people will LOVE the real you!

- Unknown

YEAH

- Read more
- cook a meal
- acheive 100% attendance
- be kind to a stranger
- clean your room
- ask a friend if they need help
- study an extra hour
- try a new hairstyle
- talk to one person outside your social group
- hug a parent
- have a digital free evening at home
- try one new food item
- say Hi to someone new!

DESTROY THIS PAGE

Bad thoughts can inhabit you for weeks if you don't deal with them. Although they can be hard to deal with, occasional bad thoughts are normal and your brain has ways of dealing with them. In this method, you can deal with negative feelings by writing them down. But what do you do when you don't want anyone to read them?

You destroy them! ✦

Life's problems wouldn't be called hurdles, if there wasn't a way to get over them.

- Unknown

Write your deepest, darkest thoughts and then destroy this page by either coloring over your writing or rip the page out and have fun destroying it in safe ways.

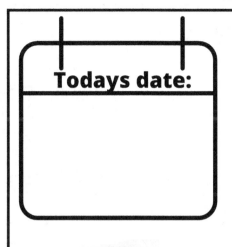

Todays date:

The next eight pages reflect my views and feelings for this past week.

What was the weather this week?

Anything exciting happen in the world this week?

Circle your emoji(s) for the week below or draw your own!

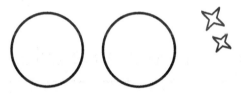

Action word of the week!

The moment I enjoyed the most -

Things to remember

Was someone kind to you?

Do you know if anyone else had similar thoughts?

To manage an anxiety attack, think of 3 things you SEE, 3 things you HEAR and finally 3 things you FEEL. Then Breathe.

Did you share your thoughts with anyone?

Were you kind to someone else?

Remind yourself that it's OK not to be perfect!
- Unknown

My best thought ....

My worst thought ....

Believe

in

YOURSELF!!

You were given this life because you are strong enough to live it.

- Unknown

WOW!

These things made me happiest this week

How can I continue to be happy?

What went wrong this week?

Everyone wants happiness.
No one wants pain.
But you can't have a rainbow, without a little rain!

- Unknown

- _____
- _____
- _____

What can I do to make next week better?

- _____
- _____
- _____

Other things to note:

Could you have changed the outcome?

Who could have shared your joy or offered support?

Did you get support when or if you needed it?

Whether the sky is blue or gray, there is something to LOVE everyday!

- Unknown

Goals for next week!

SUNDAY TUESDAY THURSDAY FRIDAY MONDAY SATURDAY WEDNESDAY

Don't change so people like you. Be yourself and the right people will LOVE the real you!

- Unknown

- Read more
- be kind to a stranger
- cook a meal
- acheive 100% attendance
- clean your room
- ask a friend if they need help
- study an extra hour
- talk to one person outside your social group
- try a new hairstyle
- hug a parent
- have a digital free evening at home
- try one new food item
- say Hi to someone new!

YEAH

DESTROY THIS PAGE

Bad thoughts can inhabit you for weeks if you don't deal with them. Although they can be hard to deal with, occasional bad thoughts are normal and your brain has ways of dealing with them. In this method, you can deal with negative feelings by writing them down. But what do you do when you don't want anyone to read them?

You destroy them!

Life's problems wouldn't be called hurdles, if there wasn't a way to get over them.

- Unknown

Write your deepest, darkest thoughts and then destroy this page by either coloring over your writing or rip the page out and have fun destroying it in safe ways.

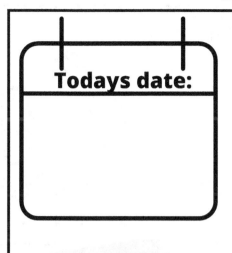

Todays date:

The next eight pages reflect my views and feelings for this past week.

What was the weather this week?

Anything exciting happen in the world this week?

Circle your emoji(s) for the week below or draw your own!

Action word of the week!

The moment I enjoyed the most -

Things to remember

Was someone kind to you?

Do you know if anyone else had similar thoughts?

To manage an anxiety attack, think of 3 things you SEE, 3 things you HEAR and finally 3 things you FEEL. Then Breathe.

Were you kind to someone else?

Did you share your thoughts with anyone?

Remind yourself that it's OK not to be perfect!
- Unknown

My best thought ....

My worst thought ....

Believe

in

YOURSELF!!

You were given this life because you are strong enough to live it.

- Unknown

WOW!

These things made me happiest this week

How can I continue to be happy?

What went wrong this week?

Everyone wants happiness.
No one wants pain.
But you can't have a rainbow, without a little rain!

— Unknown

- _____

- _____

- _____

What can I do to make next week better?

- _____

- _____

- _____

Other things to note:

Could you have changed the outcome?

Who could have shared your joy or offered support?

Did you get support when or if you needed it?

whether the sky is blue or gray, there is something to LOVE everyday!

- Unknown

Goals for next week!

SUNDAY · TUESDAY · THURSDAY · FRIDAY · MONDAY · SATURDAY · WEDNESDAY

Don't change so people like you, Be yourself and the right people will LOVE the real you!

- Unknown

- Read more
- cook a meal
- acheive 100% attendance
- clean your room
- ask a friend if they need help
- be kind to a stranger
- study an extra hour
- try a new hairstyle
- talk to one person outside your social group
- hug a parent
- have a digital free evening at home
- try one new food item
- say Hi to someone new!

YEAH

DESTROY THIS PAGE

Bad thoughts can inhabit you for weeks if you don't deal with them. Although they can be hard to deal with, occasional bad thoughts are normal and your brain has ways of dealing with them. In this method, you can deal with negative feelings by writing them down. But what do you do when you don't want anyone to read them?

You destroy them!

Life's problems wouldn't be called hurdles, if there wasn't a way to get over them.

- Unknown

Write your deepest, darkest thoughts and then destroy this page by either coloring over your writing or rip the page out and have fun destroying it in safe ways.

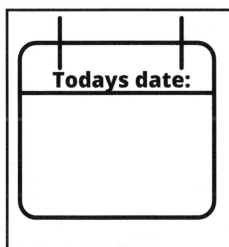

Todays date:

The next eight pages reflect my views and feelings for this past week.

What was the weather this week?

Anything exciting happen in the world this week?

Circle your emoji(s) for the week below or draw your own!

Action word of the week!

The moment I enjoyed the most -

Things to remember

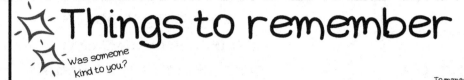

Was someone kind to you?

Do you know if anyone else had similar thoughts?

To manage an anxiety attack, think of 3 things you SEE, 3 things you HEAR and finally 3 things you FEEL. Then Breathe.

Did you share your thoughts with anyone?

Were you kind to someone else?

Remind yourself that it's OK not to be perfect!
- Unknown

My best thought ....

My worst thought ....

Believe

in

YOURSELF!!

You were given this life because you are strong enough to live it.

- Unknown

WOW!

These things made me happiest this week

How can I continue to be happy?

What went wrong this week?

Everyone wants happiness.
No one wants pain.
But you can't have a rainbow, without a little rain!
- Unknown

- _____
- _____
- _____

What can I do to make next week better?

- _____
- _____
- _____

Other things to note:

Could you have changed the outcome?

Who could have shared your joy or offered support?

Did you get support when or if you needed it?

Whether the sky is blue or gray, there is something to LOVE everyday!

- Unknown

SUNDAY TUESDAY

THURSDAY

Goals for next week!

FRIDAY

MONDAY

WEDNESDAY SATURDAY

Don't change so people like you. Be yourself and the right people will LOVE the real you!

- Unknown

- Read more
- cook a meal
- acheive 100% attendance
- clean your room
- ask a friend if they need help
- study an extra hour
- try a new hairstyle
- have a digital free evening at home
- try one new food item

- be kind to a stranger
- talk to one person outside your social group
- hug a parent
- say Hi to someone new!

YEAH

DESTROY THIS PAGE

Bad thoughts can inhabit you for weeks if you don't deal with them. Although they can be hard to deal with, occasional bad thoughts are normal and your brain has ways of dealing with them. In this method, you can deal with negative feelings by writing them down. But what do you do when you don't want anyone to read them?

You destroy them!

Life's problems wouldn't be called hurdles, if there wasn't a way to get over them.

- Unknown

Write your deepest, darkest thoughts and then destroy this page by either coloring over your writing or rip the page out and have fun destroying it in safe ways.

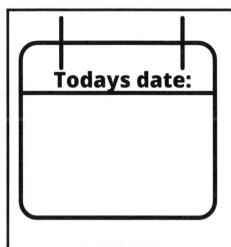

Todays date:

The next eight pages reflect my views and feelings for this past week.

What was the weather this week?

Anything exciting happen in the world this week?

Circle your emoji(s) for the week below or draw your own!

Action word of the week!

The moment I enjoyed the most -

Things to remember

Was someone kind to you?

Do you know if anyone else had similar thoughts?

To manage an anxiety attack, think of 3 things you SEE, 3 things you HEAR and finally 3 things you FEEL. Then Breathe.

Did you share your thoughts with anyone?

Were you kind to someone else?

Remind yourself that it's OK not to be perfect!
- Unknown

My best thought ....

My worst thought ....

Believe

in

YOURSELF!!

You were given this life because you are strong enough to live it.

- Unknown

WOW!

These things made me happiest this week

How can I continue to be happy?

What went wrong this week?

Everyone wants
happiness.
No one wants
pain.
But you can't
have a rainbow,
without a little
rain!
- Unknown

- _____

- _____

- _____

What can I do to make next week better?

- _____

- _____

- _____

Other things to note:

Could you have changed the outcome?

Who could have shared your joy or offered support?

Did you get support when or if you needed it?

Whether the sky is blue or gray, there is something to LOVE everyday!

- Unknown

SUNDAY   TUESDAY
THURSDAY

Goals
for next
week!

FRIDAY

MONDAY

SATURDAY

WEDNESDAY

Don't change so people like you, Be yourself and the right people will LOVE the real you!

BBB

- Unknown

- Read more
- be kind to a stranger
- cook a meal
- acheive 100% attendance
- clean your room
- ask a friend if they need help
- study an extra hour
- talk to one person outside your social group
- try a new hairstyle
- hug a parent
- have a digital free evening at home
- try one new food item
- say Hi to someone new!

YEAH

DESTROY THIS PAGE

Bad thoughts can inhabit you for weeks if you don't deal with them. Although they can be hard to deal with, occasional bad thoughts are normal and your brain has ways of dealing with them. In this method, you can deal with negative feelings by writing them down. But what do you do when you don't want anyone to read them?

You destroy them! ⟶

Life's problems wouldn't be called hurdles, if there wasn't a way to get over them.

- Unknown

Write your deepest, darkest thoughts and then destroy this page by either coloring over your writing or rip the page out and have fun destroying it in safe ways.

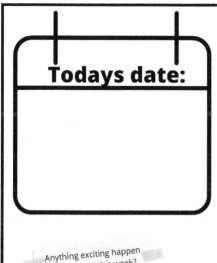

Todays date:

The next eight pages reflect my views and feelings for this past week.

What was the weather this week?

Anything exciting happen in the world this week?

Circle your emoji(s) for the week below or draw your own!

Action word of the week!

The moment I enjoyed the most -

Things to remember

Was someone kind to you?

Do you know if anyone else had similar thoughts?

To manage an anxiety attack, think of 3 things you SEE, 3 things you HEAR and finally 3 things you FEEL. Then Breathe.

Did you share your thoughts with anyone?

Were you kind to someone else?

Remind yourself that it's OK not to be perfect!
- Unknown

My best thought ....

My worst thought ....

Believe

in

YOURSELF!!

You were given this life because you are strong enough to live it.

- Unknown

WOW!

These things made me happiest this week

How can I continue to be happy?

What went wrong this week?

Everyone wants happiness.
No one wants pain.
But you can't have a rainbow, without a little rain!

- Unknown

- _____

- _____

- _____

What can I do to make next week better?

- _____

- _____

- _____

Other things to note:

Could you have changed the outcome?

Who could have shared your joy or offered support?

Did you get support when or if you needed it?

whether the sky is blue or gray, there is something to LOVE everyday!

- Unknown

Goals for next week!

SUNDAY TUESDAY THURSDAY FRIDAY MONDAY WEDNESDAY SATURDAY

Don't change so people like you, Be yourself and the right people will LOVE the real you!

- Unknown

- Read more
- cook a meal
- acheive 100% attendance
- be kind to a stranger
- clean your room
- ask a friend if they need help
- study an extra hour
- try a new hairstyle
- talk to one person outside your social group
- hug a parent
- have a digital free evening at home
- try one new food item
- say Hi to someone new!

YEAH

DESTROY THIS PAGE

Bad thoughts can inhabit you for weeks if you don't deal with them. Although they can be hard to deal with, occasional bad thoughts are normal and your brain has ways of dealing with them. In this method, you can deal with negative feelings by writing them down. But what do you do when you don't want anyone to read them?

You destroy them!

Life's problems wouldn't be called hurdles, if there wasn't a way to get over them.

— Unknown

Write your deepest, darkest thoughts and then destroy this page by either coloring over your writing or rip the page out and have fun destroying it in safe ways.

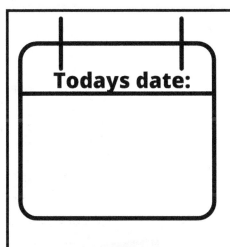

Todays date:

The next eight pages reflect my views and feelings for this past week.

What was the weather this week?

Anything exciting happen in the world this week?

Circle your emoji(s) for the week below or draw your own!

Action word of the week!

The moment I enjoyed the most –

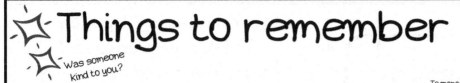

Things to remember

Do you know if anyone else had similar thoughts?

Was someone kind to you?

To manage an anxiety attack, think of 3 things you SEE, 3 things you HEAR and finally 3 things you FEEL. Then Breathe.

Did you share your thoughts with anyone?

Were you kind to someone else?

Remind yourself that it's OK not to be perfect!
- Unknown

My best thought ....

My worst thought ....

Believe

in

YOURSELF!!

You were given this life because you are strong enough to live it.

- Unknown

WOW!

These things made me happiest this week

How can I continue to be happy?

What went wrong this week?

Everyone wants happiness.
No one wants pain.
But you can't have a rainbow, without a little rain!

- Unknown

- _____

- _____

- _____

HMM...

What can I do to make next week better?

- _____

- _____

- _____

Other things to note:

Could you have changed the outcome?

Who could have shared your joy or offered support?

Did you get support when or if you needed it?

whether the sky is blue or gray, there is something to LOVE everyday!

- Unknown

SUNDAY   TUESDAY

THURSDAY

Goals for next week!

FRIDAY

MONDAY

WEDNESDAY   SATURDAY

Don't change so people like you, Be yourself and the right people will LOVE the real you!

- Unknown

YEAH

- Read more
- cook a meal
- acheive 100% attendance
- clean your room
- ask a friend if they need help
- study an extra hour
- try a new hairstyle
- have a digital free evening at home
- try one new food item

- be kind to a stranger
- talk to one person outside your social group
- hug a parent
- say Hi to someone new!

DESTROY THIS PAGE

Bad thoughts can inhabit you for weeks if you don't deal with them. Although they can be hard to deal with, occasional bad thoughts are normal and your brain has ways of dealing with them. In this method, you can deal with negative feelings by writing them down. But what do you do when you don't want anyone to read them?

You destroy them!

Life's problems wouldn't be called hurdles, if there wasn't a way to get over them.

- Unknown

Write your deepest, darkest thoughts and then destroy this page by either coloring over your writing or rip the page out and have fun destroying it in safe ways.

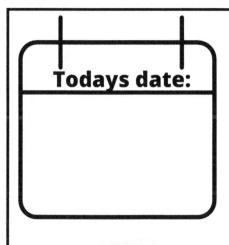

Todays date:

The next eight pages reflect my views and feelings for this past week.

What was the weather this week?

Anything exciting happen in the world this week?

Circle your emoji(s) for the week below or draw your own!

Action word of the week!

The moment I enjoyed the most -

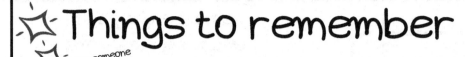

Things to remember

Was someone kind to you?

Do you know if anyone else had similar thoughts?

To manage an anxiety attack, think of 3 things you SEE, 3 things you HEAR and finally 3 things you FEEL. Then Breathe.

Did you share your thoughts with anyone?

Were you kind to someone else?

Remind yourself that it's OK not to be perfect!
- Unknown

My best thought ....

My worst thought ....

Believe

in

YOURSELF!!

You were given this life because you are strong enough to live it.

- Unknown

WOW!

These things made me happiest this week

How can I continue to be happy?

What went wrong this week?

Everyone wants happiness.
No one wants pain.
But you can't have a rainbow, without a little rain!
- Unknown

- _____

- _____

- _____

What can I do to make next week better?

- _____

- _____

- _____

Other things to note:

Could you have changed the outcome?

Who could have shared your joy or offered support?

Did you get support when or if you needed it?

Whether the sky is blue or gray, there is something to LOVE everyday!

- Unknown

SUNDAY TUESDAY THURSDAY

Goals for next week!

FRIDAY MONDAY SATURDAY WEDNESDAY

Don't change so people like you. Be yourself and the right people will LOVE the real you!

- Unknown

- Read more
- be kind to a stranger
- cook a meal
- acheive 100% attendance
- clean your room
- ask a friend if they need help
- study an extra hour
- talk to one person outside your social group
- try a new hairstyle
- hug a parent
- have a digital free evening at home
- try one new food item
- say Hi to someone new!

YEAH

DESTROY THIS PAGE

Bad thoughts can inhabit you for weeks if you don't deal with them. Although they can be hard to deal with, occasional bad thoughts are normal and your brain has ways of dealing with them. In this method, you can deal with negative feelings by writing them down. But what do you do when you don't want anyone to read them?

You destroy them!

Life's problems wouldn't be called hurdles, if there wasn't a way to get over them.

- Unknown

Write your deepest, darkest thoughts and then destroy this page by either coloring over your writing or rip the page out and have fun destroying it in safe ways.

Free Pages - color, doodle, make extra notes. Write your own comic strips!.

Be STRONG enough to stand alone, SMART enough to know when you need help and BRAVE enough to ask for it!

- by Ziad K. Abdelnour

Success is not final, failure is not fatal: it is the courage to continue that counts.

- Winston Churchill

"You are the
artist of your
life. Don't give
the paintbrush
to anyone else..

- Iva Ursano

You can't go back and change the beginning, but you can start where you are and change the ending.

- CS Lewis

Made in United States
North Haven, CT
13 July 2022

21311345R00057